GET IGNITED

Your Blueprint for Discovering
Purpose and Manifesting Dreams

BRIAN HEAT

This book is dedicated to dream chasers everywhere.
Never forget, *we* push the culture forward.

We are the visionaries.
We are the game changers.
We are the fearless.

TABLE OF CONTENTS

How to Maximize this Blueprint

Dream chasers and world changers, *Get Ignited: Your Blueprint for Discovering Purpose and Manifesting Dreams*, was written as a "spark read" intended for a fast-paced world where time is always of the essence. What you now hold in your hands is a book that is concise, content rich and filled with several easy to do strategically designed dream building activities. **In order that you properly maximize your time with** *Get Ignited*, **as you read pay very close attention to and complete the eight sections that have been graphically illustrated. The open-ended questions and recommendations found in each section, will guide you to towards uncovering your purpose and the necessary action steps you must begin working on to bring your dreams to full fruition. As you approach each section ensure that your responses and considerations are an honest depiction of who you are, what you desire and how you intend on getting there.**

Lastly, one of the strongest components of *Get Ignited* is the *Continued Growth Resource Index* I have curated at the end, which includes the most impactful literature and online inspiration I've come across in the areas of spiritual development and personal development. This index provides readers the perfect opportunity to continue their growth beyond just this book, getting them even closer to the dreams they possess in their hearts.

"The world will never encounter another you once you're gone, so with the life you've been given, make sure it's never forgotten that you were here."

Walking Phenomenon
Embracing Your True Value

Unbeknownst to most, there are over seven billion people currently living on planet Earth. What is most amazing about this fact is that within this army of souls, there are exactly no duplicates. Even among twins, where their physical appearance may seem to be identical, there are millions of tiny variations down to the molecular level that make each of them drastically unique.

This fact led me to believe that each of us, in our own right, is a *walking phenomenon*. Each one of us is a living, breathing, one-time occurrence, created with an explosive rock star rarity designed to leave an incredible impact on the world. Metaphorically speaking, we are like comets streaking across the sky but once and our calling becomes blazing a trail so bright, that it inspires generations to come long after we've gone.

Unfortunately, as many of us grow beyond our childhood years, we tend to lose our truest sense of self by spending far too much time subconsciously comparing ourselves to the lives of others. Either we find ourselves intimidated by their perceived success or incarcerated by their limited view of the world. Ultimately, transforming THEIR personal fears and biases into the bars of our own cages.

What we fail to understand is within these silent and unfair comparisons we make, when gone unnoticed, they can slowly begin to eat away at our self-worth and unique giftings, often derailing us from doing what we were born to do.

So, how do we avoid or reconcile this process? How do we, again, embrace the powerful nature of our own identity and protect our often-unimaginable divine purpose from an, at times, pessimistic world?

The answer is…we must re-dedicate our lives to the discovery of OUR OWN spiritual path, genius, and potential for greatness. We must realize that from the time we're born, the experiences that crossed our path to the family and community that influenced us, every aspect of our journey has been designed to transform who we've become and the convictions we possess. We must begin to take a more self-reflective look at every aspect of our journey. Once we do, we'll soon see that everything that's crossed our path has been leading us to discover our purpose and ultimate value to the world.

"The doorway to pursuing our dreams begins with discovering those interests and ideas that electrify our spirit."

THE RUSH

Chase What Excites You

During my own journey of reflection and self-discovery, I became intrigued with the backstories of high achievers and how they found their own passion paths. How they were able to discover their abilities then *align* themselves effectively to turn their dreams into realities.

Over the last decade, I've studied the interviews and bios of some of the highest performing influencers, fearless visionaries, and game changers around the world. Paying close attention to any reoccurring patterns I could find, I discovered the common thread in their success. When asked to describe how they found their gifts or chosen profession, each one of these high-achievers began by detailing how excited their chosen fields made them feel inside from the very beginning, as if describing love at first sight.

Each used words like "drawn to," "fulfilled by," and "captivated with" to describe what they felt when fully engaged in aspects of their craft and gifts. From the lives of professional athletes, world-renowned painters, life-changing educators and successful titans of industry, each described their passions and chosen paths as experiences or callings that gave them this incomparable internal blast of excitement.

What they described is something I like to call *the rush* – the warm and explosive physical confirmation we feel inside when immersed in those activities and conversations connected to what we were born to do. It is my belief that we possess this feeling to help us find our purpose and gifting in this world, an internal guide of sorts designed to spark our awareness and draw us closer to something greater.

Comrades, throughout my years of being an educator, mentor, inspirational speaker, and author, I've discovered that each of us have encountered these rush experiences several times as far back as our youth. However, as we grow older, many of us disconnect from who and what we truly are. We overlook the subtle *signals of destiny* our body was giving us because subconsciously, we undervalued our true power.

Disconnecting from our dream awareness most likely began at a young age when well-meaning adults belittled our imaginations by speaking negatively about what they considered the "impossibility" of our dreams. We must understand that when this occurred, these same well-meaning adults were simply projecting on us their own sense of limitations and fear hoping to "help" us avoid the possible pain or disappointment they may have faced in the pursuit of their own dreams. Of course, as young influential minds, still unsure of our own capabilities, we unknowingly believed the "advice" we were given, because we were afraid of failure and the world's criticism. So, instead of chasing what excited us, we buried these dreams deep inside, safe from risk, ridicule, and the judgment of others. This was done with such effectiveness that over time we became utterly convinced that we did not possess any dreams at all or the true ability to actually live them out. This consequence now leaves us vulnerable to walking on what I like to call the *false path*, a road in life we were never designed to take. One absent of adventure, true fulfillment, and self-determined success.

Consider what I've shared with you thus far, as you read "A Superhero's Amnesia."

A SUPER HERO'S
AMNESIA

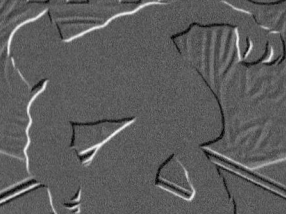

GET
IGNITED

A SUPER HERO'S
AMNESIA

What if we discovered years from now, after the sands of time slowed us down, that our true identity at birth was someone who possessed amazing superhuman abilities?

And, in losing our true identity, we settled for an unfulfilled life, verses of the adventurous one we were given.

Now, I would assume that our first reaction to rediscovering our powers would be experiencing an explosive rush of excitement...almost the feeling of being reborn!

It is my guess though, that our excitement would soon fade, if only for a moment, when we realized how much time had been wasted living far below our abilities...unable to impact the world in the most incredible ways during our most influential years.

Comrades, the true tragedy of this story is that this scenario actually plays out in the lives of millions every day. Too many of us leave this Earth without stepping into our greatest greatness. As the quote reads, "Too many people choose average when they were born extraordinary."

A Super Hero's Amnesia....

Forgotten abilities that remain dormant, and a world left absent of your unique contributions.

The world will never encounter another you

"Let your vision be your
guiding light."

BEACON IN THE STORM
Developing an Explosive Vision

Now that we've gotten a better understanding of our true value and the means by which the universe attempts to get our attention through certain feelings we experience, we now must fuse these elements together and create an explosive vision for us to follow.

What exactly do I mean when I say create an explosive vision? In a world that often surrounds us with a variety of distractions, including the ones we create ourselves, a personal vision allows us to build a captivating picture in our mind's eye that represents the ultimate life we desire to live directly connected to our gifting, convictions, and purpose.

For those of us chasing dreams and striving for our next level, developing an explosive vision is necessary to keep us inspired, focused, and on path. Crafting such a vision demands that it is emotionally exciting and represents what I like to call the *"Super Seven Vision Creators,"* or the seven key areas of an individual's life that when properly nourished and consistently strived for creates a blissful experience of fulfillment, power, and balance.

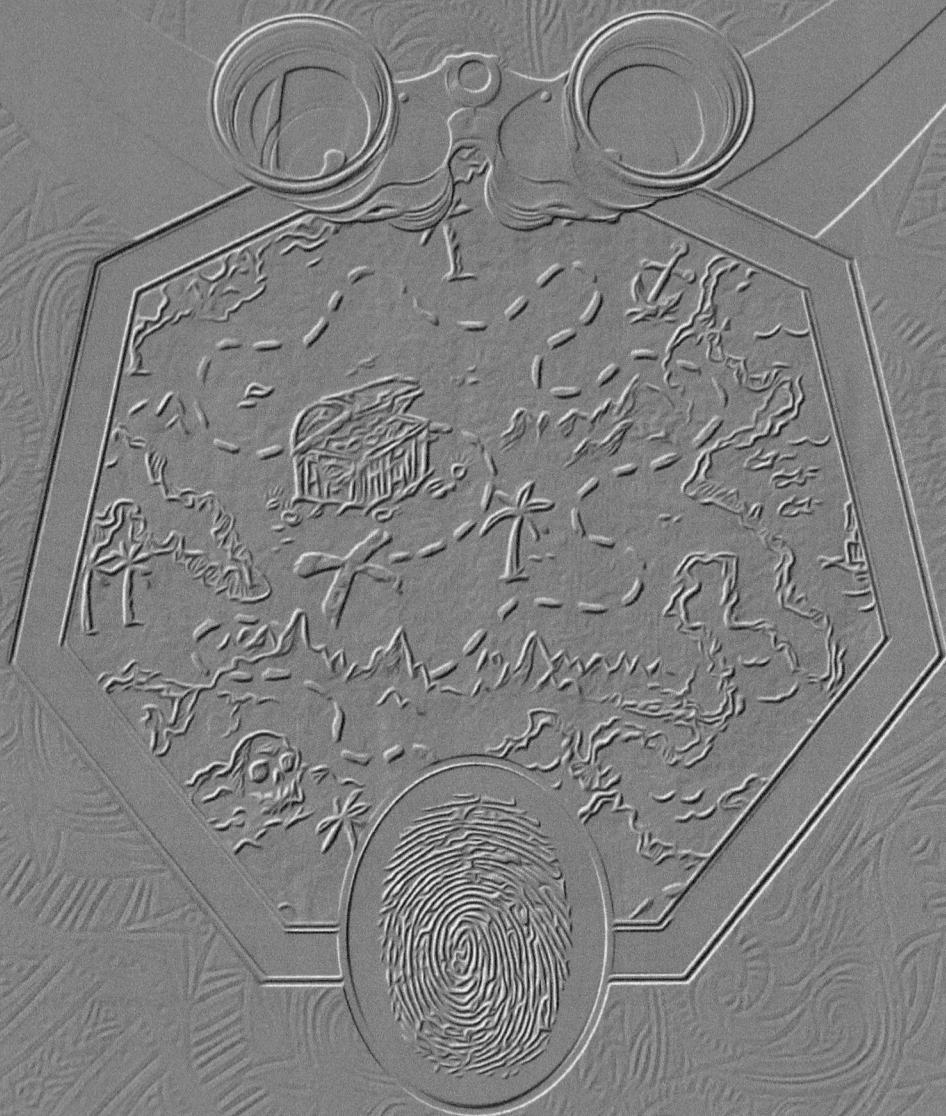

SUPER SEVEN VISION
CREATOR

Our SPIRITUAL Vision: What do we want our relationship to look and feel like with our Creator, and what role will it play in our lives?

Our PERSONAL Vision: What type of man or woman do we desire to become with regards to our character, personal growth, values/principles, and our presence in the lives of others?

Our PHYSICAL and EMOTIONAL Health Vision: What type of physical state do we see for our bodies in terms of our level of physical fitness? What type of mental soundness, joy, and emotional well-being do we want to experience daily?

Our PROFESSIONAL Vision: What career or business do we desire to invest in or redefine that is directly connected to our purpose and calling?

Our FINANCIAL Vision: What financial goals do we have connected to our earning potential, business revenue, financial literacy, debt management, credit, and assets?

Our CIRCLE OF RELATIONSHIP Vision: How do we envision the quality of our relationships within our family, romantic dealings, friends, and associates?

Our CONTRIBUTION Vision: How do we desire to give back to our communities, champion causes we care about most and philanthropic endeavors that positively impact the lives of others?

The world will never encounter another you

"Shortening the distance between you and your greatness lies only in the intensity of your desire."

CLOSING THE GAP
Determining What the Journey Will Require

N ow that we've built a masterpiece vision constructed of everything we are and everything we desire to be, the next step becomes taking a personal inventory of the necessary *skills, experiences,* and *habits* our dreams will require to come into full fruition at the level they were intended.

In order to examine our personal inventory, a useful strategy to implement is to consider our journey from a Point A to Point B perspective. Using this strategy, our goal becomes *closing the gap* between where we are and where we desire to be.

Point A is our present position in life. Here we must assess our current strengths, limitations, and resources. Simply put, who are we right now and what do we bring to the table? Now, it is essential we are very honest with ourselves during this process because if we are not, we may create a false sense of security or illusion based on unearned expertise in areas that actually need to be strengthened.

Next, we have Point B which is our desired destination, or where we would like to end up in life. *Closing the gap* becomes utilizing the necessary mindset, work ethic, strategic approach, and passion we must develop to get there. Using this thought process, we can hone in on what we must develop within ourselves to become worthy of seeing our dreams manifest.

Another strategy I've used to identify the areas of growth we must strengthen is to study those mentors, dreamers, and influencers that are leaving their own "comet like" trails blazing. Understanding from the very beginning that this is not done to copy what they've achieved or to live out THEIR unique paths, but instead to draw inspiration from how they developed their perspective gifts and carved out their own mark on the world. Greatness leaves breadcrumbs, and it is in the backstories of these high achievers that we can possibly find the missing pieces, traits, and habits they found useful stepping into their own divine light.

Study their:
Biographies
Interviews
YouTube Clips
Business Ventures
Creative Projects
Life Obstacles
Success Tips

Closing the gap is an essential step in the process where most dream chasers drop the ball. Most of us simply settle for envisioning our desires through rose-colored glasses, often living in fantasy worlds where everything we want has already been accomplished, but then lose the focus, work ethic and commitment to actually execute these same desires.

AREAS OF GROWTH
QUESTIONS

GET
IGNITED

QUESTIONS

What **experiences** do I need to increase that will bring me closer to what I desire to personally and professionally attain?

What **skills/qualifications** should I master that will improve my overall abilities to perform my craft at a high level?

What **habits** should I incorporate (or let go of) that will have a positive or self-sabotaging impact on my own growth?

"Goals are the designated targets and benchmarks we've strive to hit along the path towards personal success."

SHARPSHOOTERS
Developing and Executing Your Goals

Dream chasers, we have covered a great deal of ground re-awakening the super heroes we truly are, what we desire to do with our gifts and what growth will be required to get us there. In this chapter we will explore one of the most powerful tools utilized when looking to manifest our dreams – developing exciting goals. This process will effectively lay out a personalized game plan we can use to keep us on track, confident, and progressing forward with high octane momentum!

As you begin creating your goals, please consider the following:

How to Set Your Goals

First consider those things you want to achieve (Use the responses from your *Super Seven Vision Creator*). Then move towards designing your S.M.A.R.T goals (Specific, Measurable, Attainable, Relevant and Time-Bound). When both, your Super Seven Vision Creator and your S.M.A.R.T goals are strategically written and committed to, they will keep you motivated and focused.

Developing S.M.A.R.T Goals

Make Goals SPECIFIC:

What do you want to accomplish?
Why is this goal important?

Make Goals MEASURABLE:

How will you know when it is accomplished?

Make Goals ACHIEVABLE:

How realistic is the goal, based on your strengths, weaknesses, gifts, resources and constraints?

Make Goals RELEVANT:

Does the goal seem worthwhile?
Is this the right time to pursue this goal?
Does this goal fall in line with the direction you desire to go?

Make Goals TIME-BOUND:

When do you want this goal completed by?
What can you do today?
What can you do in a month?
What can you do in a year?

Lifetime Goals

Consider what you want to achieve in your lifetime or by a distant age in the future. Setting lifetime goals gives you the overall perspective that shapes all other aspects of your decision making.

Smaller Goals

Once you have set your lifetime goals, set a five-year plan of smaller goals that you need to compete if you are to reach your lifetime objectives.

Five Year Plan Template

Using the responses from your *Super Seven Vision Creator*, begin to formulate what necessary short and long-term goals must be achieved to see each explosive vision materialize.

What needs to be completed in the next (3–6 months)
What needs to be completed in the next (6–12 months)
What needs to be completed in the next (2-3 years)
What needs to be completed in the next (4-5 years)

KEYS TO ATTACKING
GOALS

1. Write goals down. This crystalizes them and gives them more power.

2. When you have several goals, give each a priority. This helps you to avoid feeling over whelmed, and allows you to direct your attention to the most important tasks.

3. Break goals into manageable pieces
.

4. Gather the needed resources in advance (including other people that may be required).

5. Anticipate distractions or challenges and plan for the necessary solutions.

6. Stay connected to the excitement of the overarching vision behind your goals.

7. Focus on goal execution, not simply goal creation.

Furthermore, another useful approach to have as you design your goals and move towards them is a thought process I've coined called:

Progress, Assess, and Tweak

Moving forward in life, we must keep in mind that our goals are indeed living things; not concrete, immovable objects. Goals are likely to change and evolve as we grow as individuals, but forward *progress* should always be a must. With any progress, we should always take the time to *assess* what ground we have covered and whether or not we are moving closer to our intended objectives. If we discover that we are not, we must be prepared and willing to make the necessary *tweaks* in our approach or decision making to recalibrate our efforts.

The Role Work Ethic Plays in
Goal Execution & Dream Attainment

When it comes to dream building, many people often overlook the importance of work ethic. The cliché goes…everyone desires an opportunity until it shows up looking like hard work!

The honest truth is this, you can know exactly what you want out of life and how to get there, but if you do not possess the proper mindset, hustle and dedication to stay disciplined along the journey, most of what you desire, if any, will never manifest. This is what separates the good from the great, the legendary from the forgotten and the champions from the runner ups…is their work ethic.

Characteristics of those who possess strong levels of work ethic:

Determined: You don't let obstacles stop you and you enthusiastically embrace challenges. With purpose and resiliency, you push ahead, no matter how far you have to go.

Dependable: You can be relied on to keep your promises. You are always on time and prepared for the task at hand. Your reputation for reliability precedes you because you've proven over time that clients, customers and colleagues can trust you to do everything you say you will.

Dedicated: You don't stop until the job is done and done right. "Good enough" is not good enough for you and your team. You aim for "excellence" in everything you do. You put in the extra hours to get things done right, always giving attention to every detail.

Accountable: You take personal responsibility for your actions and outcomes in every situation and avoid making excuses when things don't go as planned. You admit your mistakes and use them as learning experiences.

Respectful: You possess the power to display grace under pressure. No matter how tight the deadline or heated the tempers, you always remain poised and diplomatic. Whether you're serving a customer, meeting with a client or collaborating with a colleague, you do your best to respect everyone's opinions, especially under trying circumstances. This shows you value people's individual worth as well as their contributions.

"A collective group of excited and driven individuals pursuing a common vision is impossible to stop."

THE WINNER'S CIRCLE
Building a High-Powered Team

For many dreamers, our ambition, creativity, and rebellious natures can lead us into seasons where we are alone in our thinking and boldness of opinion. However, no matter the individual genius of our ideas, each of us must understand that it will soon take the collective efforts of a high functioning team to bring everything together.

It is understandable at the beginning of our most treasured projects that we may feel the need to keep the intimate details of what we're doing to ourselves. It allows us the necessary time to build our self-confidence and the foundational research our ideas will require. Involving too many people too soon could leave us vulnerable to toxic energy and unearned collaborations that could possible hurt the idea's natural growth. Eventually, a wise individual comes to understand that when we are aligned with the *right people* who possess expertise in key areas, in which we do not, we can begin to build a championship team to help our ideas to grow even stronger.

BUILDING AN EFFECTIVE
TEAM

GET
IGNITED

BUILDING AN EFFECTIVE
TEAM

1. The team must be led by a commonly shared overarching and inspired mission.

2. Each person's role in that mission must be directly connected to his or her own unique divine gifts and abilities.

3. Open (and honest) forums of conversation are a must to flush out new ideas and clarify misunderstandings among all team members.

4. Desired expectations must be agreed upon from the very beginning to give proper focus to establish priorities, creative vision, and effective decision-making.

The world will never encounter another you

CHARACTERISTICS OF EFFECTIVE
TEAM MEMBERS

GET
IGNITED

CHARACTERISTICS OF EFFECTIVE
TEAM MEMBERS

1. Brings their own expertise and related passion to the table.

2. Effective communicators.

3. Belief in the overarching vision.

4. Belief in collaboration.

5. Rises in the face of accountability.

6. Belief in personal growth.

7. Great problem solvers.

8. Loves to see their ideas grow stronger through the input of other team members.

The world will never encounter another you

"Learn to create where
there is nothing."

WHITE SPACES
Mastery to Innovation

As uniquely designed individuals, the universe did not intend for us to spend our days duplicating the lives and innovations of others, copying their contributions and creative impacts. Instead, we were born to venture out into the unexplored; contributing new ideas, new perspectives, and new approaches to make the world an even more exciting place for future generations to dwell in.

Years ago, I remember watching an interview with a Hip-Hop record industry executive, who was credited as one of the key figures to pioneer the genre at its inception. The interview took place on the terrace of a beautiful European villa by a reporter who was doing an expose on Modern Music Industry Moguls.

The reporter started the interview by asking how the executive was initially able to position himself at the crest of an art form that was purely an underground culture at that time. The executive responded with a smile and said, "From the beginning, I would approach club promoters, music industry executives, and investors, trying to convince them that Hip-Hop possessed the raw truth that could power a massive movement, but they just couldn't *see it*. Too stuck on what the music industry was already putting out, their minds couldn't fathom that from the inner-city streets of Bronx, New York, there would be birthed an art form built on struggle, aspirations, and honest story-telling that would one day take over the world. They couldn't see the *white spaces*." The reporter curiously asked, "*white spaces*?" The executive responded, "Yes *white spaces*. They are the gaps in EVERY industry that have yet to be explored and maximized. These are the spaces where most visionaries spend their time. This is where game changers create products, services, and ideas that shape creative revolutions. This was Hip-Hop."

From this interview, I took away what would soon become one of my core mantras in business and creativity—always look for the opportunities to create where there is nothing. Always look for *white spaces*.

From a practical perspective, I realized that in order for us to be properly prepared to redefine an industry or idea, we first need to learn how to *master the map*. By definition this means before one can innovate, one must study and master what already exists in the industry and what elements have already been "pre-drawn or pre-discovered." Before the uniqueness of our contributions get implemented, we must be fully knowledgeable of an industry's core principles and the needs that are currently being met. We must understand how the industry works inside and out, the lingo, the thought leaders in the space and what stories are being told.

Once we do this, the next step becomes *exploring the wilderness* (going beyond what's been pre-discovered), or as the executive again stated, looking for the *white spaces*. Right here, we must have the keen ability to see where the seeds of innovation can be planted. Building a better mousetrap, it is here where products like the Internet, iPods, social media, Jeremy Scott Adidas and Beats by Dre Headphones were created. After years of extensive work surrounding computer programming, digital music streaming, online social interactions, fashionable footwear, and how consumers experienced great sound quality, the individuals behind these innovations were able to make slight creative adjustments of design, function, and user experience. Creative approaches such as these allowed each of them to build new spaces in the market taking the world into exciting, unexplored directions that enhances the human experience.

But, I must warn you, developing *white spaces* is not for the faint of heart! As you begin to create innovative ideas the masses have yet to see, experience, and truly understand—just as the Hip-Hop executive attempted to the enlighten influencers early on about the potential of the genre—you may get pushback from those who don't possess the vision, intuition, and creative risk you do.

At this point, we must strengthen our convictions, ignore the naysayers, and never stop pushing the needle of progress forward, knowing with absolute belief that our unique and hard fought for contributions will one day make a difference.

"Beginning the journey to discover why you were born is the greatest adventure an individual can ever pursue."

UNLEASH THE POWER
We Were Built For More

*G*et Ignited: Your Blueprint for Discovering Purpose and Manifesting Dreams was written to spark the internal flame that each of us possess inside. This internal flame burns bright within our spirits to unleash the power of our self-worth, creativity, and value to the world.

Far too often, as it was discussed in an earlier chapter, our childlike imaginations and sense of fearlessness become confined by the taught limitations, outdated beliefs, and the personal fears of others.

Know now…we were built for more. We were born to do amazing things far beyond what the world has ever seen!

As we begin to reach the end of our time together, I ask that you keep this mind. Often when people speak of improving their "diets", they are normally referring to their eating habits. But you should know, that your true "diet" not only consist of what you eat, but also the people you allow in your circle, the visuals you take in routinely and the conversations you engage in, including your own self-talk. When looking at each of these areas combined, subconsciously they create how you interact with others, live and dream. The more positive and inspiring your "diet", the better you'll look, feel and move. But the more negative your "diet" becomes, you'll soon find manifesting your dreams extremely difficult to achieve. You must understand that all desires and personal growth require a proper "environment" in which to flourish. When we intentionally strive to ensure that everything we see, speak and do is directly aligned with our divine purpose, the world will find us impossible to stop!

Closing out, I've listed 14 Affirmations on the next page that you can begin to SPEAK daily; they will help shape your reality and re-ignite your life perspective! Each affirmation begins with the words "I AM", two of the strongest words that when combined, declare personal power over your life and how you view your own self-image. Say your affirmations with strength, say them with absolute belief...then, as your actions begin to align themselves with these new beliefs...watch how your entire world begins to change right before your eyes.

I love you and I hope your time with *Get Ignited* gave you the much needed sense of purpose and passion you were looking for! I wish you God's speed and rock star success in everything you do!

—Brian

I AM Affirmations

I AM connected to a higher power.

I AM in alignment with my highest values and principles.

I AM naturally motivated, ambitious and creative.

I AM capable of achieving anything I set my mind to.

I AM stronger than my toughest adversities and will always remain solution minded.

I AM stronger than my past, it has no power over me, because I am willing to learn, change and grow.

I AM able to turn fear into fire and push beyond my comfort zone.

I AM filled with self-love, joy and personal fulfillment.

I AM capable of forgiveness and will not hold onto resentment.

I AM accountable to my own actions and claim all consequences as my responsibility.

I AM attracted to those people, places and experiences that add value to my life and fuel to my dreams.

I AM breaking through old limiting patterns of behavior.

I AM worthy of love, kindness and respect (most of all from myself).

I AM in love with the person I am becoming.

Continued Growth Resource Index
Knowledge is Not Power, Applied Knowledge Is

Throughout my journey as a man of God, father, speaker, educator, and activist, it has never been the work of just one author, one mentor, one filmmaker, or one experience that completely defined who I would become. Instead, it was a host of books, articles, interviews, video clips, confirmations, and conversations that influenced me to renew my thinking, build my character, shape my vision, and walk through certain doors.

Get Ignited: Your Blueprint for Discovering Purpose and Manifesting Dreams was written to move your spirit into action, define who you are and where you desire to go! But, it was never intended to be the "end all, be all" of your growth and development. With that, I felt the book would be incomplete without sharing with you additional resources, authors, spiritual guides, success practitioners, and gurus who can continue pouring life into your purpose-driven journey and dream-chasing aspirations.

Spiritual Development Books

Celestine Prophecy by James Redfield
The Alchemist by Paulo Coelho
In a Pit with a Lion on a Snowy Day by Mark Batterson
The Seven Spiritual Laws of Success by Deepak Chopra
The Secret by Rhonda Byrne
The Four Agreements, by Don Miguel Ruiz
The Power of Intention, by Dr. Wayne Dyer

Personal Development Books

Think and Grow Rich by Napoleon Hill
The Magic of Thinking Big by David J. Schwartz
The 4-Hour Workweek by Timothy Ferriss
The 7 Habits of Highly Effective People by Stephen Covey
As a Man Thinketh by James Allen
Beautiful Power by Brian Heat
Mindset: The New Psychology of Success by Carol Dweck
Mastery by Robert Green
Blink by Malcolm Gladwell
Pursue Your Purpose Not Your Dreams by Dr. Joe Johnson
Mastery by Robert Greene
The 48 Laws of Power by Robert Greene
Breaking the Habit of Being Yourself by Dr. Joe Dispenza
Awaken the Giant Within by Tony Robbins

Inspiring YouTube Channels

HeatBlast TV
GaryVee
VYBO
Motivation Archive
Evan Carmichael
Live Jakes
Ted Talks
Tom Bilyeu
Law of Attraction Coaching
Team Fearless
Lisa Nichols
Words of Wisdom
Inspiring Habits
Complex's Blueprint Series

Success and Entrepreneurship Websites

www.Addicted2Success.com
(Success articles, quotes and affirmations, personal development resources)

www.Success.com
(Success articles, business profiles, entrepreneurship strategies, success resources)
www.TinyBuddha.com
(Simple wisdom for complex lives)

www.Tim.blog

(Success articles, time management, success podcasts, business strategies)
www.FranchiseHelp.com
(Franchise resources and investment opportunities)

www.Entrepreneur.com
(Entrepreneurship resources, success podcasts, entrepreneur profiles)

www.HBR.org
(Business ideas and advice for leaders)

www.SBA.gov
(Resources for launching, managing, and growing your business)

www.Ted.com
(Ideas worth spreading from today's hottest industry influencers)

www.Under30CEO.com
(Business and personal effectiveness strategies for young adults)

www.Inc.com
(Success articles, business profiles, entrepreneurship strategies, success resources)

www.GoDaddy.com
(Domain registration, website development, online marketing)

www.LegalZoom.com
(Business formation, wills and trusts, intellectual property, legal support)

www.NonProfitHub.org
(Nonprofit resources and successful nonprofit profiles)

Personal Development Podcasts

Oprah's SuperSoul Conversations
www.Oprah.com
(Soul searching interviews and self-help strategies)

The Secret to Success Podcast
www.ETInspires.com
(Personal development resources, inspiring conversations, business insights)

Eventual Millionaire
www.EventualMillionaire.com
(Career navigation, financial empowerment, business development principles)

The Art of Charm
www.TheArtOfCharm.com
(Increasing your charisma, becoming a stronger connector and reigniting your love life)

The Charged Life w/Brendon Burchard
www.Brendon.com
(Secrets to an energized, engaged, and more fulfilling life)